Soulmates:
A Collection of
Love Poems

In this book of love poems, I share my deepest feelings and emotions for soulmate connections. Each poem is a heartfelt expression of the endless love and connection one feels for their soul partner. These poems are a celebration of our love and the unbreakable bond that we share or are still looking for. I hope that through reading these poems, others will be inspired to cherish and nurture the love they have with their own soulmate.

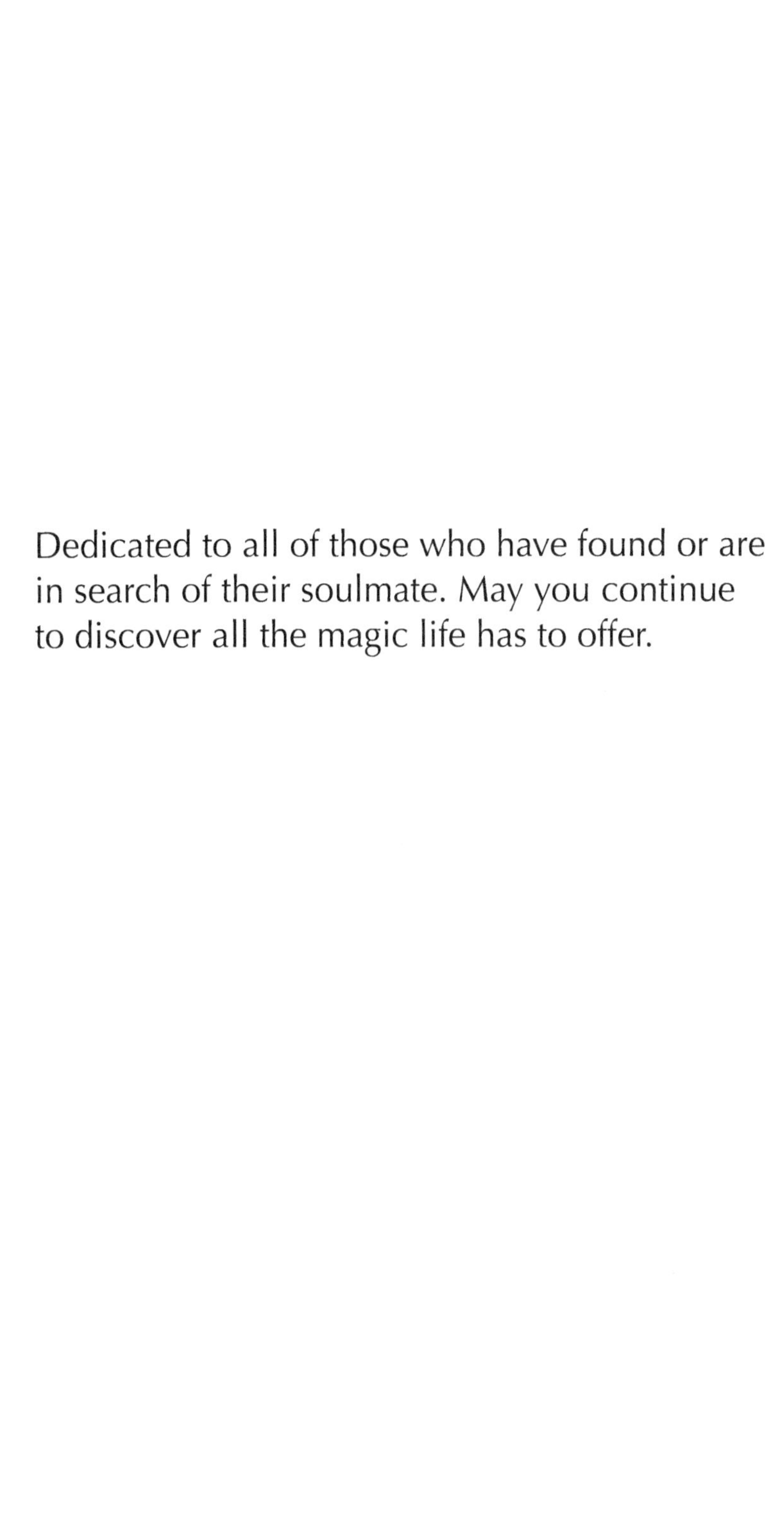

Dedicated to all of those who have found or are in search of their soulmate. May you continue to discover all the magic life has to offer.

"TO THE END"

Two soulmates, meant to be
Their love, a symphony
But roadblocks they may face
In their journey, they must brace
Through thick and thin, they will persevere
For their love, they hold it dear
Though distance may try to divide
Their bond will never subside
For they are meant to be together
Now and forever, now and forever
Through the good and the bad
Their love will never be mad
For they are soulmates, a perfect match
Their love, an unbreakable latch
They will always find their way
Together, forever, to the end of their days.

"FOREVER BOUND"

Once in a lifetime,
For some it's a fleeting glance,
For others it's a burning fire
That lasts a lifetime through.
But for the lucky few,
There comes a love
That's meant to be,
A bond so strong, so pure and true,
That even distance and time cannot break.
These are the soulmates,
The ones who are meant to be together,
Through all the ups and downs,
Through all the joy and pain.
For they have found in each other
A love that will never fade,
A love that will last forever,
Through this life and beyond.

"ETERNALLY ENTWINED"

Two souls intertwined
With hearts that beat as one
Their love so pure and true
A bond that cannot be undone

From the moment they first met
A spark was ignited
A flame that burns so bright
Their passion and love united

Through the highs and lows of life
They stand strong as one
No distance or obstacle
Can stop their fun

Their love a shining light
Guiding them through the dark
A love that is meant to be
A bond that will never mark

They are soulmates, meant to be
Their love a beautiful thing
Forever entwined, hand in hand
Their love will forever sing.

"COSMIC DANCE"

Two hearts entwined, in a cosmic dance
A bond so strong, it stands the test of chance
A love that blossoms, in the depths of our hearts
A connection so pure, it never falls apart

We are each other's missing piece
Completing the puzzle, our love will not cease
Our bond is a flame, that burns bright and true
Together we stand, against all that we do

We are soulmates, forever bound
Our love will endure, through every round
We'll face the world, hand in hand
For our love is strong, it will withstand

So here's to us, my love, our cosmic connection
I'll love you forever, with no exception.

"PUZZLE PIECE"

We are soulmates, meant to be
Our love flows deep, endlessly
Our bond is strong, our hearts are true
Together forever, me and you

We complement each other well
Our paths have crossed, a story to tell
We fit like puzzle pieces, oh so fine
Our love will last, forever divine

We share a connection, rare and pure
Our souls entwined, forever sure
We are soulmates, it's meant to be
Together forever, you and me.

"HEARTS BEAT AS ONE"

Two hearts beating as one,
A bond that can't be undone.
Destiny brought us together,
Soulmates now and forever.

Our love is strong and true,
A bond that will never skew.
No matter the distance or time,
Our love will always shine.

Inseparable, we are meant to be,
Bound by love eternally.
A love that can only grow,
Our soulmate bond, no one can overthrow.

Through the good times and bad,
Our love is never sad.
We are each other's missing piece,
Our souls forever in blissful release.

With you by my side,
I am whole and fulfilled inside.
Our love is a treasure indeed,
A bond that won't wilt like weeds.

Together, we are unstoppable, it's unmistakable,
Our love is unbreakable.
We are soulmates, meant to be,
Our love will last eternally.

"FATE'S FOREVER BOND"

Once in a lifetime,
You find that special someone,
A connection so strong,
It feels like fate has won.

Their touch, their smile,
Sends shivers down your spine,
And in their eyes,
You see forever intertwined.

With them, you feel complete,
As if every piece fits,
And through the highs and lows,
Your love never quits.

They are your soulmate,
Your partner in life,
And together, you'll conquer,
All struggles and strife.

So cherish this bond,
For it is a gift divine,
And with your soulmate by your side,
You will forever shine.

"TWO HEARTS, ONE SOUL"

Two hearts, one soul
Bound together, whole
Two minds, one thought
Together, never fought

We complete one another
Our love, like no other
Our souls entwined
Forever intertwined

Through thick and thin
We will always win
Soulmates, we are
Our love, a shining star

Together, forever
Our bond, never sever
Together our hearts sing
You are my queen, I am your king

"FOREVER SOULMATES"

My soulmate, my partner, my other half
We are bound together by an unseen force

From the moment we met, I knew you were the one
A spark ignited within my heart, and it never fades

We have been through it all, yet still stand strong
Our love grows deeper with each passing day

You complete me in a way no one else can
I am whole with you by my side

Together, we are unstoppable
Our bond is unbreakable, our love unwavering

I am grateful for you, my soulmate
You are my everything, and I am yours

Forever and always, we will be intertwined
Our souls connected, forever soulmates.

"FOREVER LOVE"

A love that's pure and true,
Two souls that were meant to be,
In this world and the next, too.

They say that soulmates are rare,
But we found each other,
A love so strong, so deep,
We know we're meant for one another.

With every kiss, every touch,
Our love only grows stronger,
A bond that's unbreakable,
We'll love each other forever.

We may have had our ups and downs,
But through it all, we stay together,
For we know that we're each other's,
Our soulmate and forever love.

"DESTINED FOR LOVE"

Soulmates, they say, are meant to be
Fate's design, a destiny
A bond so strong, it cannot break
A love that grows, with each mistake

We met by chance, on a crowded street
But something clicked, destined to meet
We talked for hours, without a care
And I knew then, you were the one to share

The road ahead, may have its twists and turns
But together, we'll conquer and learn
Through laughter and tears, we'll stand as one
Our love, a fire, that will never be undone

So here's to us, and our destined fate
May our love never dissipate
Together forever, hand in hand
Soulmates forever, in this romances that's grand.

"TOGETHER FOREVER, YOU AND ME"

Two soulmates, meant to be
Together forever, you and me
A love so strong, it never fades
A bond that deepens, as love is made

Our hearts beat as one, in perfect time
A harmony of love, so divine
We feel each other's pain and joy
A true connection, so much to enjoy

Through the ups and downs, we stand tall
Our love will conquer, through it all
We are each other's rock and shelter in any weather
In this lifetime and beyond, we'll be together

Soulmates, destined to be
Together forever, you and me.

"SOULMATE CONNECTION"

Soulmates are meant to be,
But sometimes pain comes with the key,

It's not always easy to see,
The love that was meant to be,

But when two hearts align,
It's a feeling that's hard to define,

A spark that ignites a flame,
A love that will never wane,

But even in this perfect match,
Pain can sometimes be a catch,

A hurdle to overcome,
A test of true love's strength to become,

Stronger than ever before,
And opens up the heart's door,

To a love that will never fade,
A soulmate connection that has been made,

So hold on tight, my love, through the pain and tears,
Our soulmate bond will conquer all our fears.

"SOULMATES IN PAIN"

We met as strangers,
our paths intertwined,
our souls connected,
our love defined.

But with love comes pain,
as we learned all too well,
the moments of bliss,
were quickly followed by hell.

We fought and we struggled,
our bond put to the test,
but still our love grew,
a love never at rest.

For even in the darkest times,
we held on to each other,
knowing that our souls were meant,
to be with one another.

Through all the hurt and heartache,
we never lost our way,
for our love was pure and true,
and it would never fade.

For we are soulmates,
destined to be together,
through all the joy and pain,
our love will last forever.

"COMPLETE"

With you by my side
I feel complete
Our love is a tide
That will never retreat

In your arms I find
A sense of belonging
With you, my mind
Is never alone and wandering

Our souls are intertwined
In a bond that's true
Together, we've divined
A love that's made for two

I thank the stars above
For bringing us together
I know that our love
Will last forever and ever

You are my soulmate
My partner, my friend
I feel grateful and great
Our love will never end.

"FEELS RIGHT"

My soulmate and I,
A perfect pair,
We fit together like
A puzzle with no spare.

Our love is strong and true,
A bond that can't be broken,
We face each challenge
With hearts that stay unspoken.

Through the good times and the bad,
We stand by each other's side,
Our love grows stronger every day,
A love that will never subside.

Together we are whole,
Our love is a beautiful sight,
I am grateful for my soulmate,
A love that feels just right.

"MY SOULMATE, MY FOREVER"

My soulmate, oh how sweet
You complete me, we can't be beat
Our love is strong, our bond unbreakable
Together we soar, unstoppable and unshakeable

Our hearts beat as one, our souls entwined
Our love is a flame that will never decline
With you by my side, I'm happy to my soul
My soulmate, you make my heart feel whole

Our journey together has just begun
But I know with you, I'll never be outdone
We're meant to be, our fates aligned
My soulmate, you are truly divine

I am grateful for the love we share
It's a blessing beyond compare
I thank the universe for bringing you to me
My soulmate, for eternity, yours I'll be.

"MY SHELTER"

When I met you, my soulmate,
I knew that you were meant for me.

Your touch ignites a fire within,
Your eyes sparkle like the stars above.

Together we are unstoppable,
Bound by love, we are complete.

Through the good and the bad,
We will always stand strong.

You are my rock, my shelter,
My heart and my soulmate.

I am grateful for the gift of you,
And the love we share.

You are my everything,
My soulmate, my partner,

Forever and always,
Together we will thrive.

"HOME"

Home is where you are
My soulmate, my heart
You make me feel alive
And complete in every part

When we're together, it's like
The stars align and the world has light
You are the home I've always wanted
And with you, everything feels just right

Your embrace is my safe haven
Your touch is my peace
You are my rock, my shelter
And with you, I feel your masterpiece

I am home with you
And I am grateful for each day
Because with you, my soulmate
I am truly home in every way.

"MY STAR"

Home is where you are,
My soulmate, my shining star.
In your arms I feel complete,
A love that's so damn sweet.

Together we are one,
Our bond stronger than the sun.
You bring light to my days,
And chase away all of my fears and dismay.

With you by my side,
I am no longer lost and without a guide.
You are my home, my safe place,
Where I can be myself without disgrace.

I am so grateful to have you,
My soulmate, my forever true.
Together we are home,
A love that will not roam.

"FLAMING PASSION"

My soulmate, my passion burns
In your arms, I feel alive
Our love is a wildfire, consuming
My heart with a fierce desire

Your touch ignites me,
Sparks fly and our bodies merge
In a dance of pure ecstasy
Our passion knows no bounds,
No limits to its surging force

In your embrace, I am whole
Our love a burning flame
That will never die,
But only grow stronger with time

I am forever yours, my love
And together, we will conquer all
Our passion a fiery force,
Guiding us through this wild, wondrous journey of life.

"SOULMATE LUST"

With every glance and every touch,
My lust for you grows so much.
I cannot help but crave your skin,
In your embrace, it's bliss I'm in.

Your lips are like fire, burning so bright,
With every kiss, I'm consumed by your light.
I want to taste every inch of you,
And explore every curve and every hue.

I lust for your body and your soul,
In your arms, I feel whole.
Together, we're a perfect fit,
Our passion and lust, a flame that's forever lit.

I long for your touch, your kiss,
And the way you make me feel pure bliss.
My soulmate, you are the one,
With whom I want to share this lust-filled fun.

"MY LOVE"

My soulmate, my love, my everything
You are the one that pulls my heart strings

With you by my side, I feel complete
In your arms, I find a love so sweet

Our romance blooms like a fiery flame
Never to be extinguished, always the same

Your touch ignites a passion deep within
I am yours, and you are mine, forever to win

Our love is strong and true, a bond that can't be broken
Together, we will weather any storm, unspoken

I am grateful for the gift of you, my soulmate
With you, my life is filled with love and fate.

"MY SWEET ROMANCE"

In your arms I feel at home
Where I belong and never roam
Your touch so gentle and kind
Makes my heart feel oh so fine

With every kiss and every hug cure
I feel a warmth and love so pure
You complete me like a puzzle piece
Fitting perfectly, never to release

Our love is like a sweet romance
Filled with passion, joy and dance
I am grateful for each moment we share
Knowing that with you, I found my hearts pair.

"SOLACE IN YOUR EMBRACE"

In your embrace, I find solace
A place where I am free
To be my true self, to let go
And let your love envelope me

Your arms are my refuge
A shelter from the storm
A place where I can breathe easy
And feel my worries transform

In your embrace, I feel whole
Complete and utterly alive
Your touch is like magic
A balm that heals and thrives

Your love is my treasure
A precious gift I hold dear
In your embrace, I am home
And I know you're always near

Our souls are intertwined
Bound together by fate
In your embrace, I am forever
Yours, my dearest mate.

"KISS OF THE SOULMATE"

In your kiss, I find a happy place
A safe haven in your embrace
Your lips, soft and warming
A perfect fit, like puzzle pieces forming

With every touch, a spark ignites
A flame that burns with all its might
In your kiss, I am alive
My heart beating, my soul revived

Your lips, a reminder of our connection
A bond that cannot be broken or rejected
In your kiss, I am whole
My heart yours, to have and to hold

Our souls, intertwined
Destined to be, forever entwined
In your kiss, I am home
With you, I am never alone.

"BOUND BY LOVE"

Our souls were meant to be
Bound together eternally
From the moment we first met
Our love has never been a threat

We are soulmates in love
Destined to be sent from above
Our hearts beat as one
Underneath the shining sun

We complete each other
Like puzzle pieces to one another
Our love is pure and true
And will last our whole lives through

We are soulmates in love
Our bond unbreakable, like a glove
Together forever we'll be
In each other's arms, happily

Our love is a beautiful thing
A never-ending, uplifting ring
We are soulmates in love
Blessed from the stars above.

"FOREVER ENTWINED"

Two hearts beating as one
A bond so strong, it cannot be undone
A love that flows like a river
A connection that will never quiver

Soulmates, forever entwined
A love that will never decline
Two souls, perfectly in sync
Together, forever, their bond will never shrink

Their hearts beat in harmony
A love that will last for eternity
In each other's arms, they feel complete
Their souls were meant to meet

They know that they were meant to be
This love, a destiny
Soulmates, bound by fate
Together, forever, they will elevate

Through thick and thin, they stand strong
Their love will never go wrong
Two hearts, one soul
Together, forever, they will whole.

"SOULMATES IN LOVE"

Our hearts were meant to meet
In this lifetime and beyond
For we are soulmates, my love
Bound by a love so strong

We fit together like two pieces
Of a puzzle, complete
Our souls intertwined
In a love that can't be beat

We've been through the good and bad
But our love never loses pace
For in each other's arms
We've found our happy place

Our love knows no bounds
It transcends time and space
We'll be together forever
In this love we embrace

We are soulmates, my love
Forever and always we stay
Bound by a love so strong
That nothing can ever sway.

"SOULMATES IN PASSION"

In your embrace, I am complete
Our bodies entwined, a fit so sweet
As we move together, our love on fire
Our passion igniting, a never-ending desire

In your touch, I feel alive
Electricity sparking, your body I thrive
Our lovemaking intense, our souls intertwined
In this moment, I am completely yours, and you are
completely mine

With every kiss our hearts race
Our love transcending time and space
I feel our connection, a deep and powerful bond
Our souls forever joined, our love never to be gone

In this moment, we are one
Our love burning bright, like the sun
Our bodies and souls inseparable
Together, forever, our love unbreakable.

"HOLDING ON TO HOPE"

A soulmate can be a source of great joy,
But they can also cause us pain.
In the moments when our hearts are breaking,
It's hard to remember that love is worth the risk.

But even in the midst of heartache,
We must hold on to the belief
That our soulmate is out there,
A guiding light in the darkness,
A beacon of hope and warmth.

For it is in the depths of pain
That we find the strength to persevere,
To rise above the hurt and the sorrow
And embrace the love that awaits us.

So if you're feeling lost and alone,
Remember that your soulmate is out there,
And that one day, you'll find each other
And the pain will fade away.

Hold on to the hope and the belief
That true love will always find a way,
And trust that one day, you'll be with your soulmate,
Together forever, free from pain.

"EXPLORING THE WORLD"

In your arms, I am free
To explore the world with you
From the sandy beaches
To the snowy peaks
We are unstoppable

Our love for adventure
Guides us on our journeys
Seeing new sights and sounds
Experiencing all that life has to offer

With you by my side
I am fearless and bold
Ready to take on the world
And all its wonders

Together we are unstoppable
In our quest for new experiences
Our souls are one
And our love for travel
Is boundless and infinite

I am grateful to have you
As my partner in crime
And my soulmate
In this amazing adventure
Called life.

"ADVENTURE WITH MY SOULMATE"

In a world full of adventure,
I found you by my side,
A true soulmate, a companion,
With whom I want to reside.

Together we explore the unknown,
And face the unknown with no fear,
Because with you, I feel unstoppable,
And no challenge is too severe.

We climb mountains, swim oceans,
And dance beneath the stars,
With you by my side,
I feel like I can conquer all.

In this journey of life,
You are my constant guide,
My soulmate, my adventure partner,
Forever by my side.

"LANGUAGE OF LAUGHTER"

Laughter is the sound of our souls
intertwining, a symphony of joy
that fills the air and touches our hearts

In your arms, I find solace
and a sense of belonging
that only a soulmate can provide

With every laugh, we connect
and our bond grows stronger
as we share in the happiness
of our love

Our souls dance and sing
in the bliss of our laughter
and I know that I have found
my one true love

Forever, I will cherish
the sound of your laughter
and the way it makes me feel
whole and complete

For you are my soulmate
and laughter is the language
of our forever love.

"UNBREAKABLE TEAMMATES"

Together we make a team
A perfect match, it would seem
We complement each other's strengths
And support each other's lengths

We work together, hand in hand
To reach our goals and make our plans
We face challenges and overcome
With love and trust, we're never undone

We're stronger as a unit, you and I
With you by my side, I can fly
We're a force to be reckoned with
Together, our potential like Goliath

You're my partner, worth the wait
My soulmate, my true mate
We may stumble and we may fall
But together, we stand tall

We are soulmates, a love so true
Together, our dreams come into view
We face life's challenges, side by side
Our love for each other, we can't hide

Through good times and bad, we stand strong
Our bond is unbreakable, it can't go wrong
We make a team that can't be beat
Together, our love is pure and sweet

"MY SOULMATE, MY FRIEND"

In this world of endless noise,
Of constant hustle and bustle,
I found a friend in you,
You calm my beating muscle.

Your laughter fills my heart,
Your kindness knows no bounds,
You make me feel alive,
With you, I'm never lost or found.

We share our hopes and dreams,
Our joys and sorrows too,
We know each other's deepest fears,
And help each other through.

We've been through thick and thin,
And yet, our bond remains strong,
Our friendship is a shining light,
In a world that can feel so wrong.

You are my soulmate, my friend,
The one who can make me sing,
I am grateful for your presence,
And the love and joy you bring.

So here's to our friendship,
A bond that will never break,
Together, we'll conquer the world,
It's a soulmate love, make no mistake.

"FOREVER AND ALWAYS"

Soulmates, oh how we long to find
The one who completes us, who makes our hearts beat
Who brings us joy and peace of mind
And makes our hearts and souls feel complete

In you, my soulmate, I have found
A love that is pure and true
A love that is deep and profound
And forever, I will be yours, as you will be mine too

Our souls have known each other since time began
And through every lifetime, a love that can't be measured
Our love is strong, unbreakable, and forever
For you, my soulmate, are my heart's treasure

Together, we will face whatever life may bring
And through it all, our love will continue to flourish and grow
For you are my soulmate, and I am yours
And together, we will forever be whole.

"MY PERFECT MATCH"

My soulmate, my heart's delight,
You make my world a brighter place,
With every touch, every kiss,
My love for you grows at a faster pace.

Your smile lights up my soul,
Your laughter fills my heart,
I am so grateful to have you,
As my partner in this life form the start.

We are meant to be together,
Our hearts and souls entwined,
I will love you forever,
My dearest soulmate of mine.

Our connection is unbreakable,
Our bond is strong and true,
I am yours, you are mine,
Forever, my love, I am your boo.

I am blessed to have found you,
My perfect match in every way,
I will cherish you always,
My soulmate, I love you more each day.

"FOREVER MINE"

Our souls are intertwined,
a love that's pure and true.
Like a delicate vine,
kisses with morning dew.

We are soulmates,
bound by fate.
Our love is a flame,
that will never abate.

In each other's arms,
we find our peace.
Together, we are whole,
our love will never cease.

Through all the ups and downs,
we stand by each other's side.
We are two hearts beating as one,
forever we will reside.

Our love is a treasure,
that we will always hold near.
We are soulmates,
forever, my dear.

"GUIDING LIGHT"

Our souls were once lost, wandering alone
Searching for something to call our own
And then we met, and it was clear
That we were meant to be together, my dear

You are my other half, my missing piece
The one who completes me, and brings me peace
Our love is a bond that cannot be broken
It's a love that will last, through every word, unspoken

We may have our ups and downs, but through it all
I know our love will stand tall
For you are my soulmate, my love, my life
And I will cherish you, through every moment, every strife

You are the one that touched my soul
The one who fills my heart, and makes me whole
I am so grateful, to have you by my side
You are my soulmate, my forever love, and my guide.

"MY ONE TRUE KIND"

My heart beats faster
When I'm near you
You complete me
In ways I never knew

Our souls are intertwined
Forever entwined
I knew from the start
You were my one true kind

We fit together perfectly
Like puzzle pieces
Our love is bound
By unbreakable leases

I am grateful every day
For the gift of you
My soulmate and partner
In all we do

Together, we will conquer
All life may bring
For as long as we have each other
Our love will always sing.

"A LOVE THAT TRANSCENDS"

Our souls intertwine
In a never-ending dance
Two hearts beating as one

We are meant to be
Fate has brought us together
Soulmates forever

Our connection is strong
A bond that cannot be broken
We are each other's other half

In your eyes, I see
A love that transcends time and space
Our souls are intertwined

We are two halves of a whole
Our love is pure and true
Forever bound by fate

We are soulmates, my love
Our love will stand the test of time
Together forever, till the end of time.

"DESTINED TO BE ONE"

We are two hearts that beat as one,
In love that never goes astray,
Our bond a love that's just begun,
It grows stronger with each passing day.

We face the world together,
Hand in hand, side by side,
Our love a bond that will never sever,
We'll be together 'til the day we die.

We are each other's rock,
A support through thick and thin,
Together we can weather any shock,
Our love a bond that's strong within.

Our love is a never-ending story,
A journey that's just begun,
We'll face the world with love and glory,
Together, forever, as one.

"DESTINED FOR EACH OTHER"

Our souls were meant to meet,
In this lifetime, on this earth.
We were destined to be together,
From the moment of our birth.

Our love is strong and true,
A bond that can never be broken.
We are soulmates, meant for each other,
A love that will never go unspoken.

Through the good times and the bad,
We stand by each other's side.
Our love will only grow stronger,
As we journey through life's wild ride.

We are each other's rock,
A constant source of support and strength.
We are soulmates, meant for each other,
And our love will continue to grow, to any length.

"FOUND THEIR WAY"

Soulmates, a love of pure gold,
Their love like a beacon, bright and bold.
A bond that runs deep, unspoken and true,
A love that continues to grow and renew.

In each other's eyes, they find a reflection,
Of their own hopes and dreams, their own perfection.
Through the trials and struggles, they stand as one,
Their love shining brighter than the sun.

Together they soar, higher than the sky,
Their love a guiding light, never once will die.
For when two soulmates meet, it's a beautiful thing,
A love that blossoms and forever will sing.

So here's to the soulmates, who have found their way,
May their love continue to brighten each and every day.
A love that is pure and true, a love that will last,
A love that is meant to be, forever and fast.

"BEAUTY WITHIN"

Lovers, soulmates, intertwined
Forever bound, their hearts aligned
Their love a flame that never fades
A passion strong, a bond paid in spades

In each other's arms they find their peace
A haven from the storms that never cease
They face the world with love and grace
For they know that in this life, they have found their place

Their souls entwined, a perfect match
Their love, a bond that no one can snatch
Through all the trials, they stand strong
For they know that together, they belong

Lovers, soulmates, intertwined
Their love a beacon that forever shines
A symbol of the love that never dies
A reminder of the beauty that lies within our lives.

"LOVERS AND SOULMATES"

Lovers, bound by fate and destiny
Soulmates, forever, stay with me
A bond so strong, a love so pure
Their hearts beat as one, it's love for sure

Through the highs and lows, they stand strong
Their love shining bright like the morning sun
No obstacle too great, no distance too far
Their love will conquer all, a shining star

Together they dance, beneath the moon's light
Their passion and desire, burning bright
In each other's arms, they feel complete
Their love a symphony, a never-ending beat

Lovers and soulmates, forever entwined
Their love a treasure, forever divine
Through all eternity, their hearts will remain
Bound together, in love's sweet refrain.

"BLESSED"

We searched for one another
Through the depths of time and space
Our souls connected, intertwined
In a most profound embrace

We finally found each other
After a lifetime of pleading
Our love is boundless and true
We are soulmates, our hearts beating

Through the ups and downs
We stand strong, hand in hand
Our love will never falter
We are each other's biggest fan

We are meant to be together
In this lifetime and the next one too
Our love is pure and enduring
We are soulmates, blessed and true.

"SEA OF ILLUSION"

We found each other in a sea of illusion,
in a world filled with confusion.
We were lost, but now we're found,
Together, our love is bound.

We've been through the highs and lows,
But our love continues to grow.
In each other, we've found our home,
Our hearts beat as one, never alone.

We are meant to be, our paths intertwined,
Our love is a fire that will never be denied.
We are each other's soulmate,
Our love is strong and won't abate.

We will cherish and protect,
Our love will never neglect.
Together, we'll face whatever comes our way,
For we are stronger together, forever and a day.

"HEART'S TREASURE"

Two hearts lost in the world,
Searching for their other half.
They wandered, alone and unfurled,
Hoping to find true love and laugh.

But then, one fateful day,
They found each other's soul.
Their hearts were filled with joy and glee,
They knew they were whole.

Their love was strong and true,
Never faltering, never unbending.
They knew they were meant to be,
Their love was never-ending.

Together they laughed and danced,
Their bond unbreakable and pure.
They had finally found their romance,
Their soulmate, their heart's cure.

And now they stand as one,
Their love uniting them forever.
They know they've found the perfect one,
Their soulmate, their heart's treasure.

"SING WITH ME"

Two souls intertwined
Together forever, never to part
Bound by love that is divine
Forever in each other's heart

Two hearts that beat as one
Inseparable, always together
Through the highs and lows, never done
Soulmates now and forever

The universe has brought us together
To share this amazing journey of life
Our love will last through any kind of weather
Together forever, through joy and strife

With you by my side, I feel complete
My soulmate, my partner, my everything
I am so grateful that we did meet
Together, our love will always sing.

"SENT FROM ABOVE"

Once upon a time, in a land far away,
I met the one who was meant for me that day.

Our hearts were drawn together, like two stars in the sky,
Our love for each other, was the reason why.

We were soulmates, meant to be together,
Our love for each other, would last forever.

Through the good times and the bad,
We were always there for each other, never mad.

Our love was like a never-ending flame,
Together, we were one, and never felt shame.

We were each other's rock, through thick and thin,
Our love was pure and true, and never gave in.

We were soulmates, forever meant to be,
Our love was the one thing, that set us free.

As the years went on, our love never died,
Together, we were unstoppable, and never cried.

We were soulmates, forever in love,
Together, we were one, sent from above.

"UNSTOPPABLE"

My soulmate, my love,
The one I will never quit,
Our hearts intertwined,
A perfect fit.

Your touch, your kiss,
Sends shivers down my spine,
I'm lost in your embrace,
You're my everything, divine.

Together, we're unstoppable,
Our love is unbreakable,
We'll weather any storm,
Our bond is unshakeable.

You complete me, my dear,
My soulmate, my forever,
I'll love you for eternity,
You're my one and only treasure.

"COMPLETES ME"

Once in a lifetime,
You meet someone who makes you a king.
They become your heart,
Your soulmate, your everything.

From the moment you meet,
You know you're meant to be.
A connection so strong,
It's hard to believe.

The love you share,
Is a gift God made.
It's a bond that's unbreakable,
A love that will never fade.

With each passing day,
You fall deeper in love.
And you know that this person,
Is your soulmate, sent from above.

Through the good times and the bad,
You stand by each other's side.
Because you know that together,
You can conquer anything you decide.

Your soulmate is your everything,
Your partner in life.
And with them by your side,
You're a soul-husband and soul-wife.

So here's to the one,
The person who makes your heart sing.
Your soulmate, your love,
The person who gives you wings.

"BOUND BY FATE"

Our souls were meant to be,
from the very start,
our love a cosmic symphony,
a perfect harmony of the heart.

We are two halves of a whole,
two puzzle pieces that fit,
our love like a burning coal,
that never fades or quits.

We were meant to be together,
forever entwined,
our love a never-ending tether,
that binds us so divine.

We are soulmates, my love,
forever bound by fate,
our love a gift from above,
that will never dissipate.

We will travel through this life,
hand in hand,
our love a beacon of light,
that will guide us to the end.

We are meant to be together,
forever and always,
our love a bond like no other,
that will never fade or fray.

We are soulmates, my love,
forever entwined,
our love a beautiful dove,
that will soar through all of time.

"MY REASON TO LIVE"

My soulmate, my love, my heart's delight
You complete me, you make my world bright

With each beat of my heart, I know it's true
I was meant for you, and you for me too

Your touch, your kiss, your gentle embrace
Fills me with warmth and a smile on my face

Your presence in my life has brought me peace
I am grateful to have you, my hearts newfound lease

I never knew what true love was before
But now that I have you, I want nothing more

You are my everything, my reason to live
I am yours forever, my dear and my soulmate to give.

"THE ONLY ONE"

My soulmate, my one true love
Together we soar like a dove
Our love is pure and true
I never want to be without you

Your touch, your kiss
Makes my heart beat with bliss
I am yours and you are mine
Till the end of time

With you, I am complete
My soulmate, my love, my sweet
I thank the stars above
For the gift of your love

We may have our ups and downs
But our love always stands its ground
I am so grateful to have found my sun
My soulmate, my love, my only one.

"MY SYMPHONY"

My soulmate, my love, my forever friend
Together, our hearts, forever blend

Your touch, it ignites a burning flame
In your embrace, I am never the same

With you, I am complete, I am whole
Our love, it continues to unfold

You are the missing piece to my puzzle
With you, my soul sings and it's never a scuffle

Our love is a symphony, a beautiful tune
I am grateful to have you, my soulmate, my moon

Through the good times and the bad
Our love is forever, never to be sad

You are my rock, no barricade
With you, I am never afraid

I love you more than words can express
You are my soulmate, my world, I confess.

"GUIDING ME HOME"

My soulmate, my love, my one and only,
You are the light that guides me home.
With you, I am complete,
Your touch, your kiss, your sweet embrace,
Sets my heart on fire, a burning flame.

Our love is like a symphony,
A beautiful melody that fills my soul.
With every beat of my heart,
I am drawn to you, closer and closer still.

Together, we are unstoppable,
A force to be reckoned with.
Our bond, our connection,
Is unbreakable, unshakeable, indestructible.

You are my soulmate, my love, my forever,
And I will cherish you, adore you,
Till the end of time.

"REFLECTION"

Our love is more than just physical attraction,
It's a bond that goes beyond fitting like a glove,
In the bedroom, we're completely in sync,
Our lovemaking, a perfect expression of love.

Together, we explore each other's bodies,
Finding new ways to pleasure and delight,
Our connection, deep and unbreakable,
Our love, a burning, unquenchable fight.

With every touch, every kiss, every caress,
Our passion for each other only grows,
We are one, in mind, body, and soul,
Our love, a never-ending, beautiful flow.

Our souls are intertwined, forever entwined,
Bound by a love that knows no bounds,
Our sex, a sacred, intimate act,
A reflection of the love that surrounds.

"PERFECT FIT"

In your arms I feel complete,
Our souls entwined deep inside,
Our bodies intertwined in sweet,
Passionate love that's hard to hide.

With every touch, every kiss,
I feel your love inside of me,
A love that's strong and true,
A love that's meant to be.

You are my soulmate,
My partner in crime,
Together we're unstoppable,
Until the end of time.

With you, I feel alive,
In a way I never knew so,
A love so pure and sweet,
I'll never want to let go.

In bed, we're a perfect fit,
Our bodies moving as one,
Our lovemaking is intense,
A passion that's never done.

You're my soulmate,
The one I've been searching for,
Together we'll conquer the world,
And never want for more.

"SENSUAL DANCE"

My soulmate, my love, my partner in crime
In bed, we're a perfect fit, every time

With you, I feel alive, my passion ablaze
Exploring each other, in countless ways

Our bodies entwined, in a sensual dance
Our connection so strong, it's almost trance

You're my soulmate, my forever love
Together, we rise above

In the bedroom, we're wild and free
Exploring every inch, endlessly

Our love, it burns, with a fiery flame
In each other's arms, we'll forever remain

My soulmate, my love, my partner I please
With you, I am complete, my heart on my sleeve.

"PURE BLISS"

My soulmate, you are my heart's desire
In bed, we ignite like a raging fire

Our bodies entwine, a perfect fit
As we make love, it's pure bliss

Your touch, your kiss, they drive me wild
In your arms, I feel like a child

We connect on a level beyond this earth
Our passion, more powerful than birth

Together, we are an unstoppable pair
Our love, it knows no bounds or limits of air

You are my soulmate, my partner in crime
In bed, our love is pure and divine.

"NEVER LET GO"

In your arms I find my home,
A place where love and peace both roam.

Your touch is gentle, soft and kind,
It soothes my soul, my heart and mind.

As we hold each other tight,
I feel your love, your warmth, your light.

In this moment, nothing else matters,
Only the love that we share and our constant chatter.

Our souls entwine and become one,
Together forever, till the setting sun.

I thank the universe for bringing us together,
For this love that will last forever through any weather.

In your arms, I am whole,
With you, my soulmate, my true goal.

I cherish every moment we share,
Holding each other, knowing you're always there.

With you by my side, I can face anything,
Our love will conquer all, like a beautiful symphony.

Thank you for being my best friend,
For holding me close, again and again.

I love you now and always will,
In your arms, my heart is filled.

"MAGIC WAND"

In your arms I feel safe and sound
Like a puzzle piece that's finally found
You hold me tight and never let go
A feeling that I never did know

Your embrace is warm and strong
It's where I belong
You are my partner and my friend
A love that will never end

Together we stand, hand in hand
Facing the world and all its demands
With you by my side I am complete
Our love is a force that can't be beat

In this moment I am whole
In your arms I feel your soul
I am grateful for our soulmate bond
Together, forever, like a magic wand.

"TRUE REFLECTION"

Soulmates, oh how they shine
In each other's presence they intertwine
They laugh and they play, they dance and they sing
In each other's company, their happiness rings

Their bond is unbreakable, their love is true
Together they make a team, a perfect duo
They support and they nurture, they care and they share
Their souls have found their match, they're a perfect pair

No distance or time can break their connection
Their love is strong, a true reflection
Of the joy and the happiness they find
Soulmates, oh how they shine.

"UNAFRAID"

Once upon a time, two soulmates met
And from that day on, their lives were set

They laughed and loved, and danced and sang
Their happiness knew no bounds, it seemed to never hang

Together they explored the world, hand in hand
And in each other's eyes, they found their land

They laughed at jokes, and sang silly songs
Then they cuddled up as the night grew long

They shared their dreams, and faced their fears
Together, they conquered all, and dried each other's tears

For they were soulmates, meant to be
And together, they were truly free

Their love was strong, and would never fade
For they were two halves of the same whole, forever
joined and unafraid.

"LOVE BOND"

Two hearts beating as one,
Bound together by love
They need each other
To rise above

The world may try to tear them apart
But their love is stronger, a work of art

They are soulmates, meant to be
Their love will forever set them free

When one is down, the other is there
To lift them up, to show they care

They are each other's strength and light
Together they can conquer any fight

Their love is unshakeable, indestructible,
Their bond is unbreakable, incorruptible.

Soulmates need each other, it's true
To live and thrive, to make it through

Their love will last a lifetime long
Together they will always belong.

"SOARING HIGH"

Two souls intertwined
Needing each other to survive
Completing each other's halves
Inseparable, they thrive

Together they face the world
Their love never fades
Through the good and bad
Their bond is unbreakable, never to be swayed

Their love is pure and true
A bond that cannot be broken
Without each other, they would be lost
Their love is a sacred token

They are soulmates, meant to be
Their love will never die
Together forever, they will be
Their bond soaring high in the sky.

"MEANT TO BE"

We were meant to be,
Two hearts meant to be one,
From the moment we met,
Our love was already won.

Our love was meant to be,
A bond that would never break,
We were meant to find each other,
For our love's sake.

We fit together perfectly,
Like two pieces of a puzzle, so youthful,
Our love is meant to be,
A love that's strong and truthful.

We were meant to be,
Two souls meant to be one,
Together, we'll conquer the world,
Our love, a love that's just begun.

"I MISS YOU"

I miss your touch, I miss your kiss
I miss the way you make me feel bliss
I miss the way you hold me tight
I miss you more with each passing night

I long to see your smiling face
To feel your warmth and your embrace
But until we're together again
I'll hold on tight to the end

I'll count the days, I'll count the hours
I'll hold on to the love that empowers
I'll wait for you, my love, my own
Until we're together and never alone

I miss you now and I'll miss you then
But our love will never end
It's a love that's strong and true
A love that will see us through

No matter the miles, no matter the days
I'll hold on to the love that never fades
I'll miss you now and I'll miss you then
Wishes of you is what I send.

"BURNING FLAME"

My love for you is like a burning flame
It's constant and it never wanes
I miss you more than words can say
Every second of everyday

The miles between us feel like a chasm wide
But my love for you, I can not hide
I long to hold you in my arms
To keep you safe from all harm

The thought of you brings a smile to my face
I'm filled with a warm and loving grace
I miss you more with every breath
But I know we'll be together, until death

So until the day we're reunited
I'll hold you close in my heart, ignited
A love so strong it knows no bounds
I'll love you always, my love resounds.

"SAME"

Our love is a tapestry, a work of art
Woven together with love right from the start
We feel the same, our hearts in sync
Our love, a never-ending link

We understand each other's joys and pains
We share in each other's triumphs and strains
Our love is a bond that will never break
No matter the choices we may make

Together we stand, hand in hand
Our love a beautiful and unchanging land
I feel the same, my love for you grows
Our love, a beautiful and endless rose

So let us keep our love alive
Let it flourish and thrive
I feel the same, my love for you true
Together forever, me and you.

"NEVER STRAY"

Your touch is like a pyre, a burning desire
I can't resist, it's a personal fire
Your hands on my skin, a feeling so fine
I can't help but melt, every time

Your lips on my neck, a sensual delight
I can't help but see you in sight
Your touch is electric, it sets me aglow
I never want this moment to go, it's a feeling that I know

Your hands on my body, a sensual embrace
I never want to leave this place
I crave your touch, it's my favorite drug
I never want to let go, of your loving hug

So let's get lost in this moment of bliss
Our bodies entwined, in a sensual kiss
Your touch is my addiction, I never want to stray
With you, I feel alive, in your loving array.

"CHERISH THIS LOVE"

Our paths crossed, by chance or fate
But from that moment, our love couldn't wait
We found each other, in this crazy world
Our love, a banner unfurled

We fit together, like two pieces of a puzzle
Our love, a bond that is never a hustle
We complement each other, in every way
Our love grows stronger, each and every day

We found each other, at just the right time
Our love, a beautiful and perfect design
We were meant to be, you and me
Together forever, in love, eternally

So let's cherish this love, we've found
And never let it hit the ground
We found each other, in this vast space
Our love, pure beauty and grace.

"FIRSTS"

We're doing new firsts, together as one
Our love, a beautiful and shining sun
We're exploring the world, hand in hand
Our love, a never-ending band

We're trying new things, and having a blast
Our love, a thing that will always last
We're making memories, that will never fade
Our love, a beautiful serenade

We're discovering new places, and having fun
Our love, a beautiful and shining sun
We're living life, to the fullest extent
Our love, a bond with every intent

So let's keep doing new firsts, together as one
Our love, a beautiful and shining sun
We're unstoppable, when we're by each other's side
Our love, a beautiful and endless ride.

"I F*CKING LOVE YOU"

I love you more than words can say
I love you more, with each passing day
I f*cking love you, with all my heart
Our love, a beautiful work of art

You mean everything to me, you're my world
I f*cking love you, my love is unfurled
You make me complete, you make me whole
I f*cking love you, with all my soul

I never want to be without you by my side
I f*cking love you, with all my might
You're the one for me, you're my everything
I f*cking love you, with all my being

So let's keep this love alive and well
I f*cking love you, can't you tell?
I never want to lose the feelings inside
I f*cking love you, now and forever, my love will abide.

"BEAUTIFUL SHINING SUN"

We share everything, including our food
Our love, a bond that's never crude
We taste each other's dishes, with a smile
Our love, a journey that's worth the miles

We try new recipes, together as one
Our love, a beautiful and shining sun
We share our meals, and make them a delight
Our love, a beautiful and endless light

We cook for each other, with love and care
Our love, a bond that we'll always share
We enjoy our meals, with each other's company
Our love, a beautiful and endless symphony

So let's keep sharing our meals, together as one
Our love, a beauty that weighs a ton
We'll keep tasting new flavors, and having fun
Our love, a beautiful and endless run.

"PERMANENT INK"

We got a tattoo, together as one
Our love, forever inked and won
We chose a design, that had meaning to us
Our love, beautiful and absent of fuss

We sat in the chair, side by side
Our love, a beautiful and endless ride
We held hands, as the needle did its work
Our love, a beautiful and eternal perk

We left the shop, with a smile and a kiss
Our love, a bond that we'll always miss
We have a reminder, of our love and our vow
Our love, forever inked, right here and now

So let's keep this love alive and well
Our tattoo, a symbol of our love to dwell
We'll always have each other, by our side
Our love, forever inked, a beautiful and endless ride.

"DRINK IT UP"

We drank wine, for the first time together
Our love, a beautiful and shining feather
We sipped and we savored, the flavors so fine
Our love, a beautiful and endless shine

We laughed and we talked, as the night went on
Our love, a beautiful and shining dawn
We shared this moment, just you and me
Our love, a beautiful and endless sea

We raised our glasses, in a toast to us
Our love, a beautiful and shining fuss
We clinked our glasses, and took a sip
Our love, a beautiful and endless trip

So let's keep this love alive and well
Our love, a beautiful and shining bell
We'll keep sipping wine, and having fun
Our love, a beautiful and endless run.

"BE SILLY TOGETHER"

We dance and spin, we laugh and play
We're silly, wild, and free all day
We don't take life too seriously
We just let ourselves be

We run and jump, we sing and shout
We act like kids, there's no doubt
We don't care who might see us play
We just connect in a spiritual way

We're not afraid to be ourselves
To let our love shine and reveal itself
We don't need to put on a show
We just let our love flow

We're silly, playful, and carefree
When we're together, it's clear, you'll see
That love is all we need to be
Wild, happy, and free

"SECRET CODE"

We have a secret code, just between us two
Our love, a bond that we'll always renew
We use this code, when we want to share
Our love, a beautiful and endless pair

We have inside jokes, and special phrases
Our love, a bond that will always raise
We use this code, to express our love
Our love, a beautiful and shining glove

We have our own language, that only we know
Our love, a beautiful and shining show
We use this code, to say "I love you"
Our love, a beautiful and endless view

So let's keep using our secret code, just between us two
Our love, a beautiful and shining dew
We'll keep expressing our love, in our own way
Our love, a beautiful and endless array.

"MAKE ME PEE"

We sit and laugh until we ache
Our sides are sore, our bellies shake
We tell jokes and share funny tales
We laugh so hard, we nearly fail

We laugh until our eyes water
We laugh until we start to stutter
We laugh until we have to pee
We laugh until we're completely free

We laugh and laugh and laugh some more
We laugh until we can't take it anymore
Our love is strong and full of glee
Because together, we laugh so hard we have to pee

"CHASE THE HORIZON"

We hit the road, just you and me
Our souls entwined, our hearts set free
We leave the world behind, just for a while
As we travel down endless miles

We stop to see the sights along the way
We take in all the beauty on display
We share our thoughts, our hopes, and dreams
As we chase the horizon, it seems

We're meant to be together, it's clear to see
Our love grows stronger with each mile we flee
On these road trips, our souls intertwine
And I know that you will always be mine

So let's keep traveling, you and me
Our souls united, forever free
On these road trips, our love will thrive
As we journey on, forever alive

"MY PROTECTOR"

Together, we are unstoppable
Our love is fierce and unbreakable
We stand by each other, through thick and thin
Our bond is strong, and will never end

We protect each other, with all our might
We stand as one, and fight the fight
We face the world, side by side
Our love for each other, we cannot hide

We are each other's rock, and guiding light
We keep each other safe, through day and night
Our love is unshakable, and always true
Together, we can conquer anything we do

We are soulmates, through and through
Our love is strong, and will always renew
We protect each other, with all our heart
Our love will never, ever depart

"DOORWAY TO THE SOUL"

Your eyes are the most beautiful I've seen
They sparkle and shine, like diamonds gleaming
They draw me in, with their mesmerizing gaze
I could get lost in them, for all my days

Your eyes are full of love, and understanding
They see right through me, with their demanding
I can't hide anything, when I'm in their sight
They see my soul, and all its light

Your eyes are the window to your soul
They show me who you are, and make me whole
I am grateful, every single day
That I get to see your beautiful eyes, in every way

Your eyes are my everything, and more
I am blessed, to have them to adore
They are the most beautiful I've ever seen
And I am so lucky, to call them mine, my queen

"INTOXICATING SMEEL"

Your scent is intoxicating, it's true
It draws me in, like nothing else can do
I inhale deeply, and feel my senses swirl
Your aroma, it's my favorite twirl

Your smell is unique, and all your own
It's a mixture of spices, and flowers grown
It's a blend of sweet and savory, all in one
It's a fragrance that I can't get enough of, hon

Your scent is like a drug, it's addictive and strong
It fills my senses, and carries me along
I am powerless, when I'm in its grasp
Your intoxicating smell, it's my ultimate task

Your aroma is my everything, my love
It's the one thing that I'm always thinking of
It's the scent of you, and all that you are
It's the most intoxicating smell, by far

"GAMES"

We love to play games, you and I
We have so much fun, as the time flies by
We challenge each other, to be our best
We push each other, to pass the test

We laugh and cheer, as we play along
We support each other, and sing our song
We have so much fun, when we're in the zone
We're a perfect match, and we're never alone

We play all kinds of games, it's true
We enjoy them all, and have a blast, too
We're a team, you and I
We're a force to be reckoned with, and we're always
high

We love playing games, it's clear to see
Our bond is strong, and we're meant to be
We enjoy every moment, and have so much fun
Together, we're unstoppable, when we're on the run

"A CALL AWAY"

We talked for hours on the phone,
Our connection strong and true.
I could hear the love in your voice,
And knew my heart belonged to you.

We shared our deepest secrets,
Our hopes and dreams and fears.
We laughed and we cried together,
Through all the joys and tears.

You are my soulmate,
The one I've been waiting for.
I know that our love will grow,
As we talk and laugh and explore.

So let's keep talking,
For hours on end.
Our love is a beautiful thing,
And I'm grateful we're friends.

"WORTH THE FIGHT"

We fought for our love,
Through all the ups and downs.
We never gave up,
Even when it seemed lost, it was found.

We argued and we clashed,
But always found a way to mend.
For you are my soulmate,
And I'll love you until the end.

I'll fight for our love,
With every breath I take.
I'll never give up,
For your love is all I need to make.

So let's hold on tight,
And fight for what we know is right.
Our love is worth it all,
So let's never give up the fight.

"UNSEEN FORCE"

I feel your energy,
Even when we're miles apart.
Our connection is strong,
A bond that beats within my heart.

We're twin flames,
Connected by an unseen force.
I feel your presence,
Even when we're on a different course.

Our energy intertwines,
A dance of love and light.
I know that we were meant to be,
Together forever, out of sight.

So let's embrace this connection,
This powerful bond that we share.
For our love is a flame,
That will always burn bright and fair.

"IN SYNC"

We see everything the same,
Our views and values in sync.
Our hearts and minds are aligned,
A perfect match, I think.

We share the same dreams,
And strive for the same goals.
Together, we can conquer,
Any challenge that unfolds.

You are my soulmate,
The one I've been searching for.
With you by my side,
I feel like I can do so much more.

So let's keep walking together,
Side by side and hand in hand.
With you by my side,
I feel like I can conquer any land.

"MAGNETIC"

There's a magnetic pull between us,
A force that draws us near.
I feel it in my bones,
This love that's crystal clear.

You are my soulmate,
The one I've been searching for.
Our connection is strong,
A bond that I'll always adore.

I can't resist your charms,
Your smile and your bright eyes.
I'm drawn to you like a moth,
To a flame that never dies.

So let's embrace this connection,
This powerful bond we share.
I'll love you always,
For you are my soulmate beyond compare.

"YOUR TOUCH"

I need to touch you,
To feel your skin on mine.
I crave your warmth,
And the love that intertwines.

Your touch is electric,
Sending shivers down my spine.
I never want to let go,
Of this love that's so divine.

Your embrace is like a haven,
A place where I can hide.
I never want to leave,
I"ll be right by your side.

So let's hold on tight,
And never let go.
I need you by my side,
To make my heart whole.

"CUDDLE UP"

I love cuddling with you,
Feeling your arms around me tight.
It's a feeling like no other,
A pure and perfect delight.

Your warmth and love surrounds me,
Like a blanket soft and true.
I feel so safe and loved,
When I'm snuggled up with you.

You are my soulmate,
The one I've been searching for.
I can't imagine my life,
Without this love that I adore.

So let's cuddle up close,
And never let go.
I love being with you,
In this warm and loving glow.

"WE ARE UNIQUE"

We are unique,
In our own special way.
Our love is one of a kind,
And it brightens up each day.

We have our quirks and differences,
But they only make us stronger.
Our love is something special,
A bond that lasts much longer.

You are my soulmate,
The one I've been searching for.
I'm grateful to have you by my side,
To love and to adore.

So let's embrace our uniqueness,
And all that makes us who we are.
Our love is something rare and true,
A bond as unique as a star.

"ROAD TRIPS"

They stop to gaze upon the stars,
And breathe in the cool night air.
Their lips meet in a tender kiss,
A moment they'll always share.

The car is their little world,
A place where they can be free.
And as they travel through the night,
Their love continues to be.

Their journey takes them far and wide,
To places they've never been.
But no matter where they roam,
Their love remains within.

So they stop along the way,
To soak in all that's true.
And as they kiss beneath the stars,
Their love continues to renew.

"LOVERS ON A JOURNEY"

Lovers on a journey, traveling on
Their love a beacon, shining strong
They drive through the night, their hearts ablaze
The open road before them, an endless maze

But when they stop, the passion ignites
They step out of the car, into the night
Lost in each other's embrace
Their lips meet, in a lover's race

They stand there, wrapped in each other's charms
Until the car's headlights bring them back to reality's arms
They pull apart, with a smile and a sigh
Ready to continue their journey, to the next high

Lovers on a journey, traveling far
Their love a beacon, to guide them to the stars
No matter the miles, or the stops they make
The love they share, no road could shake

"LOVERS IN THE MEADOW"

Lovers in the meadow, by a buzzing hive
The flowers in bloom, the air alive
They lay down, amidst the wildflowers
Their passion blooms, in the golden hours

The bees hum around them, a soundtrack to their love
As they entwine, they float like a dove
They give themselves, to each other completely
In the embrace, that feels so sweetly

They lose themselves, in the other's touch
As the bees fly above, in a never-ending clutch
The world falls away, as they become one
In the moment's ecstasy, their love has won

Lovers in the meadow, by a busy hive
Their love a flower, that continues to thrive
The bees may buzz, but they pay them no mind
Lost in each other, their love intertwined

"LOVERS ON A HIKE"

Lovers on a hike, through the mountains so grand
The trails winding, their hearts in hand
They take in the views, of the peaks so high
As they hike on, their love never dies

They stop to rest, by a babbling brook
Their hearts beating, with every look
They sit and talk, of the wonders they've seen
Their love growing, with each moment between

They continue on, through the forests so green
Their love a light, that guides them to the scene
They reach the summit, and take in the view
Their love stronger, than anything they knew

Lovers on a hike, through the mountains so grand
Their love a bond, that can withstand
They hike on, through the trials and the joys
Their love a constant, a beautiful poise.

"SOULMATES WHO TEXT"

Soulmates who text, all throughout the day
Their fingers flying, as they share their way
They share their thoughts, their hopes and dreams
Their hearts connected, at the seams

They text each other, from morning till night
Their love a constant, a glowing light
They share their hearts, in every message sent
Their love a bond, that can't be bent

They never tire, of the words they share
Their love a fire, that's always there
They can't get enough, of each other's touch
Their love a constant, they love so much

Soulmates who text, all throughout the day
Their love a bond, that will never fray
They share their hearts, in every message sent
Their love a constant, their souls content.

"NO MAKEUP ON"

My soulmate looks perfect, with no makeup on
Their natural beauty, shining bright and strong
They don't need paint, to bring out their glow
Their radiance shines, wherever they go

I love them just as they are, no mask or guise
Their true self, is all that I need to realize
That they are the one, meant for me
Their beauty within, is all that I see

We may not be perfect, but together we shine
Our love a light, that's always mine
We don't need makeup, to cover a flaw
Our love a bond, that's stronger than all

My soulmate looks perfect, with no makeup on
Their beauty within, is all that I don
Our love a constant, that will always thrive
Together forever, as we journey through life, alive.

"PERFECT SMILES"

Soulmates with perfect smiles, drawn to each other's mouth
Their love a bond, that stretches far and out
They smile at each other, with joy in their hearts
Their love a constant, that never departs

Their smiles are contagious, spreading light and cheer
Their love a fire, that burns bright and clear
They can't help but grin, when they're by each other's side
Their love a bond, that they can not hide

They're drawn to each other, like magnets in the night
Their love a constant, that shines bright and right
They can't get enough, of each other's perfect smile
Their love a bond, that goes the extra mile

Smiling faces, bright and true
Our love is shining through
With perfect grins from ear to ear
Our love is always clear.

"GIFTS OF FUN"

Soulmates who give funny gifts, that keep us on our toes
Their sense of humor, giving prank gifts they chose
They surprise us, with presents so absurd
Our laughter a constant, whenever we're heard

We never know, what they'll think up next
Their creativity, always something to expect
They give us gifts, that make us smile and laugh
Our love a constant, like a photograph

We try to guess, what they have in store
Our love a bond, that we can't ignore
We can't wait, to see what they'll bring
Our love a constant, a gift to make us sing

Soulmates who give funny gifts, that keep us guessing
Their sense of humor, a never-ending blessing
We love the surprises, that they bring our way
Our love a constant, every single day.

"CRAVE YOUR SKIN"

Sitting next to each other, the need to touch is strong
Our love a constant, that can't go wrong
We sit together, entranced by each other's gaze
Our love a constant, in so many ways

We don't need words, to express our love
Our hearts speaking, from up above
We reach out and touch, our fingers entwined
Our love a bond, that's intertwined

We need to feel, each other's love and care
Our hearts afire, with love to share
Sitting next to each other, the desire to touch is clear
Our love a constant, that we hold dear

We crave the feeling, of each other's skin
Our hearts beating, with love within.

"THEIR LOVE A CONSTANT"

They don't care, what others may think or say
Their love a constant, in every single way
They laugh and play, in the open air
Their love a constant, without a care

They dance and sing, like no one's watching
Their love a bond, that's never halting
They embrace the looks, that others give
Their love a constant, as long as they live

They just enjoy, each other's company
Their love a bond, that's meant to be
They laugh and play, without a worry
Their love a constant, in no hurry.

They are silly, in public together
Their love a bond, that will last forever
They don't care, what others may think
Their love a constant, that never shrinks.

"YOUR BEAUTY WITHIN"

You are beautiful, inside and out
Your soul shining, with love no doubt
Your beauty within, radiates so bright
It's a constant joy, to be in your sight

Your outer beauty, is a sight to behold
But it's your inner beauty, that never grows old
Your kindness and love, are things to treasure
Your beauty within, is a beautiful pleasure

You are beautiful, inside and out
Your love a constant, without a doubt
Your beauty within, is something to see
Your love a constant, that sets you free

You are beautiful, inside and out
Your love a constant, without a doubt
Your beauty within, is a joy to behold
Your love a constant, that will never grow old.

"I'M ENOUGH"

With you by my side, I feel like I'm enough
Your love a constant, that's oh so tough
You believe in me, and all that I can be
Your love a constant, that sets me free

You accept me, just as I am
Your love a constant, that's always grand
You support me, in all that I do
Your love a constant, that's always true

You encourage me, to be the best I can be
Your love a constant, that gives me wings to be free
You inspire me, to be my true self
Your love a constant, that gives me wealth

With you by my side, I feel like I'm worthy and loved
Your love a constant, from up above
You make me feel, like I'm a love vessel
Your love a constant, that I don't wrestle.

"LOST WITHOUT YOU"

I feel lost and alone, without you by my side
Your love a constant, that I can't hide
You are my anchor, in stormy seas
Your love a constant, that sets me at ease

You are my compass, when I'm unsure
Your love a constant, that's always pure
You guide me, through life's twists and turns
Your love a constant, that always burns

I feel adrift and lost, when you're not around
Your love a constant, that keeps me on ground
You are my rock, in troubled times
Your love a constant, that always shines

You are my soulmate, my one true love
Your love a constant, that I'm always thinking of
Without you, I feel lost and alone
Your love a constant, that's my home.

"KISS ME"

Kissing you is like a dream come true,
A feeling that I can't help but pursue
Your lips are soft and full of life,
A treasure I am lucky to have as my wife

Every time we lock lips,
I am filled with a feeling of pure eclipse
Your kisses are like a warm embrace,
A comfort I can always count on in any place

I could kiss you all day,
Never tire of the joy and the play
For when I am with you,
I am truly alive, my love forever true

So let us continue to kiss and love,
And cherish every moment we share, up above.

"I'M WAITING FOR YOU"

I feel so alone in this crowded room,
Surrounded by people, yet feeling consumed
By a loneliness that seems to grow
With every passing moment, every ebb and flow.

I long for someone to hold me close,
To whisper sweet words and banish my woes.
But as I stand here, all by myself,
I can't help but wonder if anyone else
Feels this same sense of isolation,
This unshakable feeling of desolation.

But even as the tears begin to fall,
I hold onto hope, standing tall.
For I know that one day, someone will share my soul,
To fill this empty space, to make me whole,
And until then, I'll keep standing strong,
Believing that love and companionship belong
In my life, even when I feel alone.

"MAKING LOVE"

Making love to you is like a beautiful dance,
A tantalizing tango of passion and romance.

Your body is a canvas, a work of art,
A place that fills me with joy and heart.

Every time we come together,
It's like the first time, a beautiful tether
Of passion and pleasure, love and lust.
Making love to you is a must,
A need that I can't resist,
A feeling that I can't dismiss.

Your touch is electric, your kisses sweet,
A feeling that can't be beat.

So let us continue to love as a pair,
And cherish every moment we share,
For when we're together, the world falls away,
And all that matters is the love we create, forever and a day.

"I MISS THEE"

Oh, how I miss thee when thou art away,
My heart doth ache with each and every day.

The thought of thee fills me with such despair,
A longing so strong, it's almost unfair.

I pace the floor and count the hours,
Till thou art by my side and bring me flowers,
To fill this emptiness within my soul,
To fill me up, to make me whole.

But even in thy absence, I am not alone,
For thy love surrounds me, a love that's grown
From a seed of affection, into a mighty tree,
A love that will last, eternally.

So though we may be miles apart,
Our love remains strong, beating in our hearts,
A love that will bring us back together,
Forever and a day, now and forever.

"THOU ART MY EVERYTHING"

Thou art my everything, my heart doth say,
Without thee, my world would surely stray.

I need thy touch, thy love, thy kiss,
To fill this emptiness I cannot dismiss.

Thou art the light that guides my way,
The one that makes my heart feel less gray.

I need thy strength to face each day,
Thy support to help me find my way.

Together, we are stronger, more complete,
Our love a bond that can't be beat.

So let us hold on tight, my love, my hun,
And never let go, for we are one,
Our love a force that will conquer all,
Now and forever, through every wall.

"THROUGH THE AGES"

Roses are red, violets are blue,
My love for you grows more each day, it's true.

You are the one that makes my heart skip a beat,
The one that makes my soul feel complete.

Your touch is electric, your kisses sweet,
A feeling that can't be beat.

Together, we are like two peas in a pod,
Our love a bond that can't be broken or flawed.

So let us hold on tight and never let go,
For our love is a beautiful rose that continues to grow,
A love that will last through the ages,
Now and forever, through all life's phases.

"GENTLE BREEZE"

Roses are red, violets are blue,
I am so grateful to be loved by you.

Your love is like a rose in bloom,
A beautiful sight that fills my room.

Your kisses are sweeter than any wine,
A feeling that is simply divine.

Your touch is like a gentle breeze,
A comfort that never fails to please.

So let us hold on tight, my hun,
And never let go, for we are one,
Our love a force that will conquer all,
Now and forever, through every fall.

"NOW AND FOREVER, BLISSFULLY"

Thine eyes do sparkle like the stars above,
Thine lips do speak of endless love.

Thine touch is gentle, yet electric,
Thine embrace is a feeling I cannot neglect.

I crave thee like the flowers crave the sun,
Thine love is a warmth that can never be undone.

Thou art my everything, my heart doth say,
Without thee, my world would surely stray.

I need thy touch, thy love, thy kiss,
To fill this emptiness I cannot dismiss.

So let us hold each other close, my mate,
And never let go, for we are connected by fate,
Our love a force that will set us free,
Now and forever, blissfully.

"NEVER ENDING"

Lovers entwined hearts beat as one,
Eternal flames of love, forever won.

In each other's arms, they find their peace,
Their love a never-ending release.

Together they stand, strong and true,
Their love forever, a sight to view.

"HERE TO STAY"

Lovers, entwined in a bond of love,
Their hearts beating as one, like a dove.

Their love is a flame that never fades,
A light that guides them through life's shades.

In each other's arms, they find their peace,
Their love a never-ending release.

Together they stand, strong and true,
Their love forever, a sight to view.

They face the world hand in hand,
Their love a force that can withstand
Any challenge that comes their way,
For their love is here to stay.

"SOULFULLY"

Soulfully, we are drawn to each other,
Our love a force that can't be smothered.
Out of all the people in the world,
Love brought us together, our hearts unfurled.
Making a life with you is all I crave,
Together, we stand, strong and brave.
Time has no power over our love,
Endlessly, we will rise above.
As long as we have each other,
True happiness, we'll discover.

"I SEARCHED"

I searched high and I searched low,
For a love that would never go.
I searched near and I searched far,
For a love that would be my shining star.

I searched in the city and in the countryside,
For a love that would be my perfect guide.
But no matter where I looked, I couldn't find,
The love that would make my heart entwine.

Then one day, I found you, my love,
And everything fell into place like a glove.
You were the one I had been searching for,
The love that I love to my core.

Now I know that I will never again roam,
For with you, my love, I've found a home.

"O LOVER"

O lover, thou art cute and funny,
Thy love for me, oh so sunny.
Thy smile lights up my day,
In thy arms, I am here to stay.

Thy touch is gentle, yet electric,
Thy embrace a feeling I cannot neglect.
Thy kisses are sweeter than any wine,
A feeling that is simply divine.

Thou art the light that guides my way,
The one that makes my heart feel gay.
Together, we are stronger, more complete,
Our love a bond that can't be beat.

O lover, thou art loving and true,
I am grateful to be loved by you.
Our love will last through all of time,
A bond that is truly one of a kind.

"DANCE AND LAUGH"

Lovers, we play and laugh together,
Our love a bond that will last forever.
Your touch is gentle, your embrace so sweet,
A feeling that's loves retreat.

We dance through life, hand in hand,
Our love a force that can withstand
Any challenge that comes our way,
For our love is here to stay.

We laugh and play, our hearts aglow,
Our love a flame that will never slow.
Lovers, we are meant to be,
Our hearts and souls forever free.

We'll dance and laugh, until the end of time,
Our love a love that is truly divine.

"SWING WITH ME"

Lovers in a hammock, swaying in the breeze,
Our hearts at ease, as we kiss in trees.
Adventure awaits, just around the bend,
Our love a force that will never end.

We'll explore the world, hand in hand,
Our love a bond that can withstand
Any challenge that comes our way,
For our love is here to stay.

In the hammock, we'll dream and play,
Our love a love that will never stray.
Lovers, we are meant to be,
Our hearts and souls forever free.

We'll adventure and explore, until the end of time,
Our love a love that is truly divine.

"THEIR LOVE FOR EACH OTHER"

Two soulmates in love, their hearts aflame
They share a bond that can't be tamed
Through songs and melodies, their love is growing
Their bond so strong, it just keeps on flowing

They dance to the beat of their own drum
Their love for each other, it never goes numb
They share their secrets and their deepest fears
Their love for each other, it never veers

Their bond is deep, it cuts to the bone
Their love for each other, it never has flown
They share their songs, their joy and their pain
Their love for each other, it always remains

So here's to the soulmates, who love and share songs
Their love for each other, it just keeps going strong
Their bond so pure, it can't be denied
Their love for each other, it will never subside

"SCREEN TIME"

Together we sit, laughing until we cry
Watching funny videos, oh how time does fly
We share in the joy and the humor all through the night
Our bond so strong, it was love at first sight

We can't help but giggle, at the silly things we see
Our love for each other, it just keeps growing exponentially
We hold hands and cuddle, as we watch the screen
Our love for each other, it's always serene

We share in the laughter, the jokes and the fun
Our love for each other, it has just begun
We'll watch funny videos, until the end of time
Our love for each other, it will always shine

So here's to us, soulmates and best friends
Our love for each other, it never has to end
We'll watch funny videos, until the stars go out
Our love for each other, it's what love is about

"A STRING ACROSS THE UNIVERSE"

Like a string that stretches across the universe,
Our connection is strong and unbreakable.
No matter where we are, no matter how far,
Our love remains unshakable.

We are bound together, heart to heart,
By an unseen force that can't be denied.
No distance can tear us apart,
Our love is a flame that will never subside.

Though galaxies may come between us,
And time may pass us by,
Our love will endure,
A constant, shining light in the sky.

So let the universe do its worst,
For our love will stand the test of time.
For you and I are connected,
Like a string that stretches across the cosmos, intertwined.

"COSMIC CONNECTION"

Our love is a cosmic connection,
A force that transcends space and time.
No matter where we are in the universe,
Our hearts are forever intertwined.

We are two stars, burning bright,
Orbiting around each other in a never-ending dance.
Our love is a force that unites,
A bond that can never be torn asunder by circumstance.

Together we are unstoppable,
A supernova of love that shines bright.
For our love is a cosmic force,
A connection that will last through the night.

So let the universe do its worst,
For our love will stand the test of time.
For you and I are connected,
By a cosmic force that is truly divine.

"CAN'T TEAR US APART"

Our love is a wildfire, burning bright,
A flame that can never be named.
We can't keep our hands off each other,
In a love that is both wild and untamed.

Every touch is electric,
Every kiss a spark that ignites.
Our love is a force that is unstoppable,
A bond that is both fierce and tight.

We are two magnets, drawn together,
Unable to resist the pull.
Our love is a love that is all-consuming,
A desire that is insatiable and full.

So let the world try to tear us apart,
For our love is a force that cannot be denied.
For you and I are connected,
In a love that is wild, passionate and tried.

"AGELESS LOVE"

Our love is a love that defies the ages,
A bond that knows no bounds.
We are soulmates, you and I,
In a love that is profound.

Though our years may be different,
Our hearts beat as one.
Our love is a love that is timeless,
A bond that has already won.

We are two parts of a whole,
Completing each other in every way.
Our love is a love that knows no limits,
A bond that will forever stay.

So let the world try to tear us apart,
For our love is a force that cannot be denied.
For you and I are soulmates,
Connected by a love that will never subside.

"DIFFERENT LIVES"

Our love is a love that knows no bounds,
A bond that transcends time and space.
Though our lives may be different,
Our souls are forever entwined in a loving embrace.

We are two halves of a whole,
Completing each other in every way.
Our love is a love that knows no limits,
A bond that will never fray.

We may live different lives,
But our love remains the same.
A constant, burning flame,
That will never be tamed or contained.

We will never part,
For our love is a force that cannot be denied.
For you and I are soulmates,
Connected by a love that knows no bounds, forever
intertwined.

"TANTRIC CONNECTION"

Our love is a tantric connection,
A bond that goes beyond the physical.
We are one in body, mind, and soul,
In a dance that is both spiritual and sensual.

Together we move as one,
In a rhythm that is both slow and fast.
Our love is a never-ending dance,
A bond that will forever last.

We are two halves of a whole,
Completing each other in every way.
Our love is a tantric union,
A connection that will never stray.

So let the world try to tear us apart,
For our love is a force that cannot be denied.
For you and I are connected,
In a tantric bond that will always thrive.

"I WAS LOST"

I was lost, wandering through life,
Never knowing what love could be.
But then you came into my world,
And everything was made clear to me.

You showed me what it means to love,
To open my heart and let you in.
With you by my side, I feel complete,
My soul finally able to begin.

Our love is a love that knows no bounds,
A bond that will never fade.
You are my soulmate, my one true love,
The missing piece that my heart has made.

So let the world try to tear us apart,
For our love is a force that cannot be denied.
For you and I are meant to be,
Together forever, a love multiplied.

"KNOWS NO BOUNDS"

Our love is a love that knows no bounds,
A bond that is strong and true.
We are soulmates, you and I,
In a love that is meant to anew.

We love to travel and explore,
To see the world and all its wonder.
Together we are unstoppable,
Our love growing stronger and fonder.

But we also cherish our alone time,
The moments where it's just you and me.
For in those moments, we can be ourselves,
And our love can flourish and be free.

You and I are soulmates,
For our love is a force that will never die.
Connected by a love that knows no bounds,
A love that will always fly.

"TIME"

We've found each other, we're soulmates true
A love that runs deep, forever new
But sometimes we need a little space
To be alone, to find our own place

We understand each other, so well it seems
We don't need words, our love redeems
The moments apart, they make us stronger
When we come back, we love longer

Feels new, it's been tested and tried
Our love, it has survived
The need for alone time, it's okay
Our love will always find its way

So go ahead, take some time alone
I'll be here waiting, when you come home
Our love, it will thrive, it's here to stay
No distance, no time, can keep us at bay.

"MY BEST FREIND"

You're more than just my lover, you're my best friend
Our bond, it goes beyond, until the very end
We laugh and we cry, we face life's ups and downs
Together, we'll conquer, any obstacle we've found

We share secrets and dreams, we support one another
Through thick and thin, we stand together, like no other
We're not just soulmates, our friendship runs deep
Our love, it grows stronger, as we fall asleep

In each other's arms, we find peace and calm
With you by my side, I can face any harm
You're my rock, my shelter, my guiding light
Together, we'll make it through, day and night

So here's to us, my soulmate and friend
May our love and friendship, never meet its end.

"MY PERSON"

You're my person, the one I turn to
In good times and bad, I know what to do
I call you up, and you're always there
With a listening ear, and a love so rare

You understand me, like no one else can
You accept me, just the way I am
You lift me up, when I'm feeling down
You turn my frown, into a smile so bright and profound

I am so grateful, to have you in my life
My soulmate, my partner, my constant spirit wife
Through every challenge, we stand side by side
Together, we'll conquer, and always abide

So here's to us, my love, my person
May our bond, forever be unbroken and certain.

"HAPPY"

I see the way you smile, when you're feeling glad
It lights up your face, and it's oh so rad
I want to be the one, to bring that joy to you
To see you happy, it's all I want to do

You make me happy, just by being you
Your quirks and your imperfections, they make me love you too
I want to return the favor, in any way I can
I want to be the one, who makes you understand

That you are loved, more than words can say
I want to show you, in every single way
That you are special, and you mean the world to me
I want to make you happy, for eternity

So here's to us, my love, my happiness
I'll do anything, to bring a smile to your face, no less.

"MY OBSESSION"

I can't stop thinking about you, my love
You're always on my mind, from up above
I want to be with you, every moment of the day
I want to feel your touch, in every single way

I crave your presence, like a thirst that can't be quenched
I need your love, it's the only thing that's left
I can't get enough, of your sweet embrace
I am addicted, to your loving face

I know it's obsessive, this love of mine
But I can't help it, it's just so fine
I need you with me, to feel complete
You're the missing piece, the one I can't delete

So here's to us, my love, my obsession
I'll love you forever, with no hesitation.

"AFFECTIONATE LOVE"

Your touch is gentle, your embrace so sweet
It fills my heart, with love so complete
Your kisses, they set my soul on fire
I am yours, my love, my one desire

You make me feel, like the luckiest of all
To have your love, it's worth standing tall
Through every challenge, we stand side by side
Together, we'll conquer, with love as our guide

Your affection, it means the world to me
It's a feeling, that I never want to be free
I want to hold you, and never let you go
I want to show you, my love that's bound to grow

So here's to us, my love, my affection
I'll love you forever, with all my heart's direction.

"KNOWN YOU FOREVER"

I feel like I've known you, for all of time
Our bond, it's so strong, it's truly divine
We connect on a level, that's hard to explain
It's like we've known each other, through every single pain

We finish each other's sentences, and know what the other means
We share the same thoughts, and chase the same dreams
We're so in sync, it's like we're one mind
Our love, it's a bond, that's truly intertwined

We belong together, there's no doubt in my mind
You're my soulmate, my partner, my one and only kind
I'm so grateful, to have you as my best friend
Our love, it's a treasure, that will transcend

So here's to us, my love, our soulmate connection
I'll love you forever, with no exceptions.

"ENDURE"

Our love, it endures, through thick and thin
It stands the test of time, and always wins
We've been through so much, but we're still here
Our love, it grows stronger, year after year

We've faced challenges, and we've overcome
We've learned and grown, through every moment of fun
We've built a life, that's full of love and light
Together, we've found, our peace ever night

Our love, it's a flame, that will never die
It's a bond that's unbreakable, high up in the sky
It's a promise, we've made, to be together
Through every storm, and every kind of weather

So here's to us, my love, our endurance
I'll love you forever, with no interference.

"FLIRTY CONNECTION"

We flirt with each other, all the time
It's a playful game, that's always on my mind
I love the way you smile, when I make you laugh
I love the way you blush, when I make a pass

We can't keep our hands off each other, it's true
Our attraction, it's electric, it always feels new
We can't resist, the chemistry we share
It's a love, that's beyond compare

We're soulmates, destined to be together
Our love, it's a bond, that will weather
Every storm, and every sunny day
We're meant to be, in every single way

So here's to us, my love, our flirty connection
I'll love you forever, we are perfection.

"MY REFLECTION"

You are my reflection, my other half
You complete me, in every single laugh
I see myself, in your loving eyes
I am at home, I know you feel likewise

You understand me, like no one else can
You know my heart, and all my plans
I am myself, when I am with you
I am free, to be who I am meant too

Together, we're a perfect match
Our love, it's a bond, that we'll never detach
We fit together, like two puzzle pieces
Our love, it never ceases

So here's to us, my love, our reflection
I'll love you forever, with no deflection.

"SELFLESS LOVE"

Our love, it's selfless, it's pure and true
It's not about me, it's all about you
I put your needs, before my own
I want to make you happy, and never be alone

I love you, for who you are, inside and out
I support you, through every self-doubt
I'm here for you, through every single trial
I'll be by your side, and always make you smile

I cherish you, and all that you do
I'm grateful, to have a love that's so true
I'll always love you, more than you know
You're my soulmate, I will never let go

So here's to us, my love, our selfless devotion
I'll love you forever, with our harmonic motion.

FOR YOU…

To all the lovers out there,
Who have found their other half.
May your love continue to thrive and flourish,
And never falter or collapse.

To those who have searched for their soulmate,
And finally found their perfect match.
May your love continue to be great,
And never fade or detach.

To those who have been through the hardships,
And have fought to keep their love alive.
May your bond continue to be steadfast,
And never be torn or deprived.

To those who have found their happily ever after,
And are living their dream.
May your love continue to flourish and prosper,
And never be silenced or gleam.

Here's to all the lovers,
May your love continue to thrive.
May you always be each other's shelter,
And never be apart or contrive.

UNTIL WE MEET AGAIN…